Wildland Wildfires

and Where the Wildlife Go

Riverfeet Press

108.5 West Callender St.

Livingston, MT 59047

www.riverfeetpress.com

WILDLAND WILDFIRES

and Where the wildlife go

Randie Adams

Children's book

Copyright 2018 © by the author

Edited by Daniel J. Rice

All rights reserved.

ISBN-13: 978-1732496897

This title is available at a special discount to booksellers and libraries.

Send inquiries to: riverfeetpress@gmail.com

Design/Layout by Daniel J. Rice

Pine cone & Deer track illustrations by Timothy Goodwin

Color Illustrations by Randie Adams

Dedicated to:

Dr. Clayton Marlow

There once was a time when forest fires were not put out, but instead accepted as part of nature. These fires that affected the forests came naturally by lightning, and sometimes were even used as a tool to manage the surroundings. Fires would come and go in all different sizes and strengths, leaving behind amazing places for the wildlife to live. Most commonly there would be patches within the forests and the grasslands that would burn. It was not very often that all of the trees would disappear.

The year following a fire, in the vast open grasslands, young nutritious grass grew and thrived. The eager young bison led by their wise mothers would frolic and play among the new and exciting vegetation, following the path where the greenest and sweetest grasses grew best.

Closer to the forest, where the sagebrush grew strong, the grassland birds hopped along. If grasses had been grazed and weren't overly thick, it was likely the fire would not spread too quick. The patches that burned, whether small or big, gave a special purpose for each little egg.

The handsome males loved to strut in the open, while the mothers used shrubs to hide their young and protect them. As the little chicks grew they learned how to feed on the insects, like the fast grasshopper, who liked areas where sagebrush may not be the thickest.

If too much sagebrush had burned, the antelope would move along as snow fluttered down to cover the ground in a white, fluffy blanket. When the snow later melted the antelope would return, finding shrubs that had started to regrow. These were perfect for their spring and summer munching as they zipped back and forth over the hills.

The deer would not care so much and just give a sigh. They would move along keeping this place in the back of their mind. Maybe sometime later, in 10 years or so, after the shrubs grew much bigger this place would be perfect for them to roam. For now, they would make their home in an unburned forest, moving near a willow-covered stream.

Small fires can clean the forest floor of fallen trees and logs. The tree-tops that were untouched left shelter for the elk from weather and predators. A new path was now open helping them feel more at ease as they moved freely from forest to meadow.

The year after a much larger fire, young grasses and forbs would sprout. Elk came to these areas in an excited hurry. This new vegetation was one of their favorites that they would not want to waste.

If a fire came through that was big and strong enough to burn all the large mother trees, the Black-backed woodpecker would come to live. Only in places like this would he be pleased. The bark that had burned made the little bugs easier to find and catch. Yes, a heavily burned area was his paradise even though other animals may not have thought so.

The moose, a solitary old grump, traveled with each season. In the summer he trampled through wet meadows and willows. In the winter he went higher where old and young trees were both plentiful, eating on branches that were easily within his reach.

If a fire came through where his summer home was, the following year he'd be happy with the new growth, "Younger grasses and shrubs taste better anyway." His winter home though, was a very different story. If a fire burned the smaller trees, he would go hungry and become angry.

A few years after a fire had passed through, rabbits would be present. New shrubs had already started to grow, the perfect place for hiding and making a home. It wasn't too thick but enough to keep them safe. Coyotes and foxes would follow these rabbits, and were always trying to play a game of hide and seek.

Bears, like the rabbits, came back within a few years. Some of those same shrubs that the rabbits used for hiding, had berries that were perfect for fall feasting. The roots of the forbs, like biscuit-root and fireweed, were all around for the summer. He also liked meat and would find what he could, protecting his meal from all that came by. He liked to stay to himself and his area was large. Land that had burned or not, had its individual charm.

No forest fire is the same, there is no doubt about that. The size of a fire will always be different. Some trees have seeds that need the heat a fire brings, to break free and be able to grow. Other trees take longer to regrow and will struggle as they try their best to reach the sky. Animals know how to use the land they live on. They will move and adjust, making the best of what nature gives them.

Now that more people live closer to the forests, fires have been put out quicker. This is done to protect our homes, but it also brings changes to what the forest had known. The fires that had been controlled made them fewer and smaller. More plants and trees grew bigger and took over. Like adding logs to a campfire, this added more fuel to the forest making those fires more dangerous.

Remember, while science has shown a forest fire can make different homes for many different animals, a fire at the wrong time of year or one that becomes much too strong, can set the forest back and take longer to return it to what it had once been. There are brave men and women who work very hard and know how to use fire like a tool. Fire should never be played with and must be respected. A natural fire, like those started by lightning, does not have to be quite so scary.

Other titles from Riverfeet Press

THIS SIDE OF A WILDERNESS: A Novel (2013)
- Daniel J. Rice

THE UNPEOPLED SEASON: Journal from a North Country Wilderness (2014)
- Daniel J. Rice

WITHIN THESE WOODS: A collection of Northwoods nature essays with original illustrations by the author (2015) - Timothy Goodwin

RELENTLESS: A Striker Mystery Novel (2015)
- Marcus Bruning & Jen Wright

ECOLOGICAL IDENTITY: Finding Your Place in a Biological World (2016)
- Timothy Goodwin

TEACHERS IN THE FOREST: Essays from the last wilderness in Mississippi Headwaters country (2016)
- Barry Babcock

ROAD TO PONEMAH: The Teachings of Larry Stillday (2016)
- Michael Meuers

A FIELD GUIDE TO LOSING YOUR FRIENDS: Essays on Loss (2017)
- Tyler Dunning

AWAKE IN THE WORLD: A Riverfeet Press Anthology (2017) - various authors

ONE-SENTENCE JOURNAL: Short Poems & Essays from the World at Large (2018) - Chris La Tray

YOUNG BUT FREE: A Novel (coming soon)
- Daniel J. rice

I PAY ATTENTION: A collection of five children's books about the senses (coming soon) - Erika Baily-Johnson

www.riverfeetpress.com

38396756R00020

Made in the USA
Columbia, SC
06 December 2018